Monet.

PARK
LANE

"Claude Monet fought to catch the fleeting sensation, to put down on his canvas light and shimmering water: to stop time."

Claude Oscar Monet was born in Paris, November 14th, 1840 to a modest family of shop-keepers. His father Claude-Auguste was the owner of a grocery store on the outskirts of town. It was evidently not a flourishing business, for in 1845 the family moved to Le Havre, and Auguste Monet went to work with his brother-in-law.

Claude (Monet was called Oscar as a boy and it is the name with which he signed his first canvases) revealed a natural talent for drawing very early. His school notebooks are filled with sketches and caricatures of his teachers and school friends. Later, his quick pencil found favour with the local well-to-do citizens. His somewhat bizarre and slightly satirical caricatures pleased them and he earned as much as ten francs apiece for a drawing, sometimes even more.

At first Monet drew mostly to amuse himself, although it was not from lack of talent. Eventually, however, his love of drawing led him to pursue it more seriously and he began to take lessons from such drawing masters as Ochard, a disciple of David, who recognised the unusual gift of his pupil early on.

Another master, Eugène Boudin, showed even more interest in the young Claude, offering him friendship and encouragement. He helped the young artist with his studies and urged him to apply himself harder. "Your work is very good for a beginner," he told him, "but you will soon have had enough of it. Study, learn to see and to paint, to draw and to do landscapes." These were words that would make a strong impression on the young man, even though at first he stubbornly continued to work on his caricatures. "Why," said Claude to himself, "should I give up work that I enjoy and with which I can make money easily to do something new — painting — with which I may not make any money at all?"

Thus filled with doubts, Monet began to paint. His teacher Boudin often took him on long walks and the two delighted in the luminous atmosphere they discovered outdoors, with its new tonalities.

It was at this point that Monet began to focus on colour as the most important element of a painting.

From an artistic point of view, those years were decisive. He would later say of that period: "... I truly understood nature and I also learned to love it."

In 1859 Monet, the young man from the provinces, decided to take on Paris, the capital of art and home of the Salon, embracing it with youthful enthusiasm. His father had tried to obtain a scholarship for him from the municipal authorities in Le Havre, but it had proved to be in vain. So Claude arrived in Paris, a city bursting with intense cultural activity at the time, with only a small allowance from his

Asters, 1880. Private collection

father and his own savings earned from the work he had done as a caricaturist.

Young Monet had several attractive qualities in his favour, however: he was a good-looking young man of medium height and he exuded a joie de vivre and great resolution. He made friends quickly and was soon familiar with all the important artistic debates raging at the time. Surrounded by heated discussions, Monet would sit scribbling caricatures on the corner of a table in the Brasserie des Martyrs to pay for his meals there, profiting from everything he saw and heard around him. The painter Troyon received him with kindness and encouraged him to study the figure and particularly, the nude. Following his advice, Monet began to work at the Académie Suisse, and there he met the painter Camille Pissarro who had already exhibited at the Salon.

However, young Claude had no intention of spending all his time studying at the Académie and Monet's father, seeing that his son purposely chose to remain on the fringes of the circles around the great painters, refused to send him more money.

After his first visit to Paris in the spring of 1861, Monet did his military service in Algeria. However, he began to suffer problems with his health, and was forced to return to France for good the following year. There he again took up with his old friends and once more threw himself into the work he had grown to love most, painting. He looked up his old friend Boudin who was always ready to offer help and advice. He also met the painter Jongkind, a shy Dutchman whom Monet liked instinctively. Monet said of him: "From that moment on, he was my true teacher. It is to him that I owe the real education of my eye." This enthusiastic group of young artists rambled the countryside around Le Havre, painting in meadows, in gardens, and along the beaches, anywhere there was light and colour to be found.

In autumn 1862 Monet returned to Paris and to please his father, he began to go regularly to the studio of Marc-Charles-Gabriel Gleyre. There he met the painters Bazille, Renoir and Sisley. But his restless nature did not allow him to remain at Gleyre's studio for long. He soon left Paris for Chailly, a village in the middle of the Fontainebleau forest. There, wandering the forest paths and smelling the strong scent of the trees, he experienced the exultant sense of freedom he loved so much. Solitude and the rhythms of nature suited his temperament and stimulated his visual imagination and creativity; there, he observed, he drew, he painted. It was a happy period for the artist. Although he was only twenty-six, Monet's friends already considered him a master.

Once he had painted all that interested him around Chailly, Monet moved on with his friend Bazille to a place near Honfleur, on the road to Trouville. It was May 1864. Each day Monet's discovery of new subjects to paint filled him with a desire to express what he saw and felt on canvas. He painted numerous works inspired by the countryside around him: the road in front of the farm where he took his meals, the shipyards around Honfleur, the estuary of the Seine.

Except for a few portraits painted out-of-doors, landscapes were his favourite motif.

In 1865, with help from his father, who had never stopped believing in his son's talent, Monet rented a small studio in Paris with his friend Bazille. There, while waiting for the opening of the Salon, he put the finishing touches on two paintings that he planned to submit to that year's exhibition. The paintings were accepted and that year the *Gazette des Beaux-Arts* included a new name, that of Mr. Claude Monet.

The two works that he showed, *The Seine Estuary* and *Bridge over the Hève at Low Tide*, were a success, with some declaring that they brought new light and a breath of fresh air to the Salon. A few visitors who had not heard of Monet even confused him with Manet, who was not all pleased to find himself praised for someone else's work. The day after the opening of the Salon, Monet returned to Chailly. There, filled with fresh enthusiasm, he began his own version of *Luncheon on the Grass* which he finished in his studio in Paris. However, it was not among the works he submitted to the Salon of 1866. Instead, he submitted two others, *Camille*, or *The Green Dress* and *The Forest at Fontainebleau*, both favourably received by the critics, especially the first, which portrayed the woman who would eventually become Monet's wife. These paintings also won him the friendship of Manet and enthusiastic criticism from Emile Zola.

His success at the Salon seemed to fill Monet with new energy and he began to sketch the first canvases for a series of views of Paris that he finished the following year.

Back in Ville-d'Avray, Monet tried something new: a canvas painted completely out-of-doors, portraying four women in a garden. The model for all of them was his mistress, Camille. The painting *Women in the Garden*, was of such large dimensions that the artist had to dig out a trench for it in the ground, making the trench progressively deeper as he worked so he could reach the upper parts of the canvas. He probably did not finish the work out-of-doors where he started it, but this had no effect on its quality. Unfortunately, however, the painting was refused by the jury of the 1867 Salon.

Monet's financial situation grew worse and he left Ville-d'Avray, hounded by creditors. He sought refuge first in Sainte-Adresse in Normandy, and then in Honfleur where he resumed his painting with intensity. Some relief from his concern over money was offered by the ever-generous Frédéric Bazille who bought from him *Women in the Garden*, which Monet had just finished, paying him 2,500 francs in monthly installments. However, poverty continued to haunt Monet and the situation grew more serious after Camille gave birth to their first child. Little Jean, "a big beautiful boy" was born August 8th, 1867. Monet was overjoyed but his financial worries continued to be pressing. He needed to earn at least enough to feed his family. Added to his worries about money were a natural restlessness and a constant anxiety to do more and better work. Looking for new places to inspire him, he returned to Sainte-Adresse. There he painted several seascapes, some gardens and the regattas in Le Havre.

Monet's financial situation continued to be a precarious one. He

The Beach at Trouville, 1870. Private collection

harassed Bazille with ever more urgent and bold requests for money, sometimes to the point of being offensive. Bazille helped as much as he could, but he often reproached Monet for his ingratitude. It was only later, after young Frédéric Bazille had died in the war, that Monet would remember with affection and recognition the man who had helped him so much.

During this difficult period, another painting of Monet's, *Ship Leaving the Docks of Le Havre*, was accepted by the Salon of 1868. One critic demolished it completely. However, another painting *Fishing Boats* was more successful, receiving a silver medal in the International Maritime Exhibition in Le Havre for its "indisputable sincerity of execution".

In the following years, 1869 and 1870, Monet's paintings were refused by the Salon. It was a rude shock for the artist, but, with the encouragement of Boudin and his own unwavering self-confidence, Monet began to work anew. One generous patron, a Monsieur Gaudibert, helped him to find new quarters near Paris where, even though he did not always have enough to eat, he could at least work in peace. The painter Renoir was a close friend of Monet's at the time, and one result of this friendship was the famous *Grenouillères* paintings they did, working side by side.

Throughout all this, Camille, the mother of his son, remained loyally by his side, sharing his years of misery. They eventually married, on June 28th, 1870 in Paris.

That same year the Franco-Prussian war broke out. The war years were to be difficult ones for the French and many artists left France, seeking refuge in England for the duration of the war. Among those who left were Monet and his family who moved to London. Unhappily, the time they spent there was often miserable and lonely.

In London, the artist worked out-of-doors, painting the bridges over the Thames and the gothic cathedrals in the English fog. He also visited museums with another refugee, Pissarro, and met the art dealer Paul Durand-Ruel, for whom he began to work.

The following year he returned to the continent and visited Holland. That country charmed him and he stopped for a time in Zaandam, painting the countryside with a sure eye, capturing on canvas the colours he saw. One result was a painting *Windmill near Zaandam*, dated 1871. The sojourn in Holland was an enriching one for Monet, although more in terms of experience than money. When he returned to France after the war and after the Commune, he brought back many studies with him. However, after the death of his father, he no longer found Le Havre a place of refuge. He moved instead to Argenteuil, a place that pleased the keen eye of the artist, with its river that widened into a basin, its promenade planted with trees that were reflected in the water, its many flower gardens, and upstream, the bridges over the Seine.

Monet was fascinated by his new home, as indeed were many of the Impressionists who made it one of the landscapes most often painted by them. Among others, Sisley, Manet and Renoir often joined their friend there to work.

It was around Argenteuil that he painted many of his most famous works, such as *Regatta at Argenteuil*, *The Railway Bridge at Argenteuil*, *The Bridge at Argenteuil*, and *The Studio-Boat at Argenteuil*. The artist spent many happy hours painting on the banks of the river and in the light and colour-filled gardens. The two paintings, *Camille Monet at the Window, Argenteuil* of 1873 and *The Family in the Garden at Argenteuil*, of 1875 are marvellous examples of the work he did there in those years, fairylands of reds, greens and blues.

Fresh inspiration came with a return visit to Holland. In Amsterdam, Monet's palette took on a new chromatic range, like "a harp with chords of light". His canvases acquired a different kind of luminosity, a feeling of light that brought them to life. Monet experimented with the division of tones, using small touches of pure colour juxtaposed next to each other, thereby portraying light with a new vibrancy which he had not been able to achieve before simply by mixing colours on his palette.

This technique, which was one open to debate, was also used by Monet in another canvas, a seascape painted in Le Havre. He called it *Impression, Sunrise* and displayed it on April 15th, 1874 at a collective exhibition. The name was seized upon by a critic, who jeeringly used it in an article entitled "Exhibition of the Impressionists".
The name stuck.

Nevertheless, success, or at least a tangible expression of it, was still not in hand. Although he stayed in Argenteuil, Monet was forced to move to an even more modest house. His resources were almost at an end, with the inheritance he had received from his father and his wife's dowry spent. Luckily for him, at this point Monet met a rich businessman, Monsieur Hoschédé, who helped him financially for a short time and bought some of his canvases. But by 1878, riddled with debts, the painter was forced to leave Argenteuil. Monet and his family moved once again to Paris where his wife gave birth to their second child, Michel. Even in the grey capital, however, Monet found light and colour to paint. That year his work *Rue Saint-Denis, National Holiday* portrayed the street colourfully decked out for the "fête nationale" on June 30th.

But Monet did not stay in Paris long. His patron Hoschédé went bankrupt and Monet suffered the effects of his loss. In an attempt to help Monet with what little remained to him, Hoschédé invited Monet and his family to share the Hoschédé house in Vétheuil, downstream from Mantes on the Seine. The two families lived there together during the autumn of 1878. The situation, however, was a delicate one, for Monet was not insensitive to the charms of his benefactor's wife. The situation grew worse when Monet's wife Camille fell ill; she died soon after, leaving behind two small children.

Monet assuaged his grief by throwing himself into his work and painting with a desperate eagerness. He did a number of still-lifes and painted the famous *The Break-up of the Ice near vetheuil*, the result of a cold harsh winter along the Seine. To those who asked to see his studio, Monet would point to the hills, fields and the frozen Seine next to a Vétheuil white with snow and would reply: "There is my studio." This was what gave birth to the myth that Monet was a painter who worked exclusively out-of-doors, although his studio work still played an important though imprecise role in his painting.

In June 1880 the review "La Vie Moderne" organised an exhibition of Monet's work and sales were surprisingly good. For a short time, Monet's financial worries were eased. With the good weather, his canvases were again filled with their old luminosity; he painted *Spring* and *The Apple Orchard at Vétheuil* full of green reflections and yellow vibrations of light.

At the end of 1881 Monet left Vétheuil for Poissy, half-way between Vétheuil and Paris, but by the end of 1883, the artist had again moved, this time to the village of Giverny in the province of Normandy in the north of France. It was a pleasant village nestled among the hills, in a valley where the Epte meets the Seine.

"I expect to paint masterpieces here for I like this countryside very much," he wrote to a friend.

That great river, the Seine, attracted him as much as ever. He followed it through fields and pastures and along banks lined with poplars. It was an ideal landscape for the enchanted eyes of the artist. Monet had a large cabin built on a boat, similar to his boat-studio in Argenteuil, and he floated it up and down the river, painting the streams, the meadows bordered with willows and poplars, the haystacks in the fields, the orchards and the gardens. But even the enchanted landscape of Giverny could not hold the painter's attention for long, his search for new motifs led him ever onwards to new places. And so we find him in Etretat on the Manche in northern France, Belle-Île on the Atlantic, Antibes on the Côte-d'Azur and in Bordighera on the Italian Riviera. In most places, his stay was short, but he arrived in Bordighera in January 1884 and remained there for a longer period. We know a great deal about this sojourn from the extensive correspondence he carried on with Madame Hoschédé, who had become his confident. "You must know once and for all that you and my children are my whole life," he wrote to her, " ... and every motif that I do ... I say to myself I must do it well so that you can see where I have been and what it is like here."

Monet did not lack for motifs in Bordighera, yet his painting produced in him mixed feelings of serenity and despair: serenity for the incomparable beauty of the spot, and despair, because the painter feared he would not be able to capture the light of the countryside surrounding him. "At times I am frightened out of my wits by the tones that I must use ... the light is terrible," he wrote in one letter. Later, however, he wrote: "I feel good here now, I dare to put down the red and blue tones; it is a fairyland, it is delightful and I hope it will please you."

In April that year, 1884, Monet went back to Giverny and resumed his old life, but it was not yet to be a smooth one. There were to be still more years of difficulties and problems ahead as he continued to be tormented by moral crises and anguish, sometimes to the point where he would lose all interest in painting.

This ambiguity lasted until the death of Mr Hoschédé in 1891. The following year, in July 1892, Claude Monet and Alice Hoschédé were married.

After that, the artist's life became more serene and this was reflected in his painting. Monet again took up his studies of composition, which he called "series". As the light constantly changed the appearance of the landscapes and objects he was trying to paint, he had to execute his motifs quickly to capture what was essential about them and put this down on his canvas.

Here is how Monet explained it: "I started to paint some haystacks that had caught my attention earlier. They formed a magnificent group, not two steps from here. Then I saw that the light had changed. I told my step-daughter to run to the house and kindly bring me another canvas. She brought it but shortly after that the light was different again. So I said: 'Another! Bring me another!' And I did not work on any of them unless the effect was just right. That's all. It's not very difficult to understand."

This procedure of doing a series became his method of work. The famous series of paintings of the cathedrals at Rouen, painted between 1892 and 1894, are testimony to it. The most beautiful creations of the artist's final period were mostly painted around Giverny, with the exception of a trip to Norway and a stay in Venice in 1908 where he painted delicate arabesques of churches and palaces on the Grand Canal, one of which, *The Church of Santa Maria della Salute, Venice*, seems almost to rise out of the sparkling water.

But it was in France in his beloved village in Normandy that Monet painted his charming canvases *Water Lilies* in 1899. They were the first of his paintings to portray the famous pond which the painter had had dug in his garden at the edge of his land, and had filled with water channeled in from the Epte. The pond, with its small Japanese-style bridge, its flowering wisteria and superb water lilies, was the unquestionable protagonist in the master's paintings of that period.

By 1903, even though he continued to paint with great intensity, he concentrated all his attention on the simple surface of the pond, with its delicately-coloured water lilies floating on the water. When these paintings — forty-nine canvases of *Water Lilies* in all — were shown in May 1909 at the gallery of the art-dealer Paul Durand-Ruel whom the Monet had met in London, success suddenly burst upon him.

No longer was Monet the impoverished painter of works that no one wanted to buy. Now he was a name on the lips of every critic.

Inevitably, just as success and celebrity finally caught up with him, along came more unhappiness. Monet had suffered problems with his vision for many years and now it grew worse. Blindness became a real threat.

Added to this concern was the grief he felt upon the death of his second wife Alice who had never recovered from the loss of one of her daughters. After a short illness, she died in 1911.

This new and cruel blow was so devastating that for a time Monet seemed to lose all interest in life. Even painting no longer gave him comfort.

A difficult year passed. Then a new exhibition of twenty-nine of his canvases was held in Venice at the Galerie Bernheim, bringing fresh attention to the elderly painter.

However, it was the friendship of an influential man of politics, Georges Clémenceau, that brought him out of his despondency. This ardent Frenchman, a republican with many literary and artistic interests, gave comfort to Monet in his last years. Clémenceau took an interest in the unhappy old painter, writing to him encouragingly, and urging him not to dwell on his troubles. In a letter written in 1912 he writes: "You are not threatened with losing your sight at all ... you must believe that the cataract of your bad eye will soon be 'ripe' and then they can operate."

Clémenceau urged him to go back and finish a project that Monet had abandoned following the decline in his health. It was a project particularly close to Monet's heart. The artist had thought of using the motif of his *Water Lilies* to decorate the whole Salon, and to paint it so as to give the illusion of one endless painting.

Encouraged by Clémenceau's interest, Monet decided to build a large studio at Giverny where, on a kind of portable easel, he installed canvases on a chassis more than 4 metres wide and 2 metres high. Monet sat in front of this enormous rolling easel, and using studies of the motif he had drawn in happier times, he calmly painted his pond, with its marvellous water lilies bathed in the light of a delicate sunset.

Work on the great canvases of *Water Lilies* continued throughout World War One. At the end of the conflict, to celebrate the victory of 1918, Monet offered his work to the French people; his old friend Clémenceau, who was now Premier, acted as intermediary. Even though Monet had not yet finished the panels, the French government, as an act of recognition, offered him a large sum for his painting *Women in the Garden*, exhibited at the Orangerie of the Louvre.

It was the culmination of Monet's career, not only for himself as a man, but also as a painter and as the last great survivor of Impressionism. In 1923, the frenetic activity of the artist came to a halt. Monet was almost blind and doctors operated successfully on his right eye, which had been harder hit than his left. Finally, in 1925, the year before his death, he could write that he was "... working hard and with unequalled joy."

He was able to finish his last great work. To the illustrious visitors who came to see it, he presented *Water Lilies* in the order in which it would be displayed in the Salon's rotunda.

At last, on December 6th, 1926 the eyes that had captured such light and colour while Monet was alive, closed forever.

In the end, there was no official ceremony nor solemn funeral for the artist. Instead a simple homage was paid by the inhabitants of Giverny to their Monsieur Monet.

1. Shipyard near Honfleur - 1864. Private collection - *This was one of the first important works painted by Monet, a result of his formative experience in Normandy with Jongkind, Boudin and Courbet. In this work, Monet's instinctive feel for the effects of light remains within the framework of traditional concepts as is his use of colour.*

2. Luncheon on the Grass (detail from the left half) - 1866. Musée d'Orsay, Paris - *This work, with its life-sized figures, marks an important stage in the Impressionist evolution of Monet. Begun in Chailly in 1865, Monet devoted long hours to the elaboration of the theme. He made many studies for it, fearing that the large-scale of the painting would destroy the freshness of the composition.*

3. Camille or The Green Dress - 1866. Kunsthalle, Bremen - *For this portrait of his mistress Camille Doncieux, Monet was awarded a prize at the Salon of 1866, winning his first important critical and public success. The delicate play of light on the folds of the dress, caught in a single moment, seems to make the portrait come alive.*

4. The Church of Saint-Germain-l'Auxerrois, Paris - 1867 (dated 1866). Nationalgalerie, Charlottenburg, West Berlin - *Surprisingly enough, this painting was done inside the Louvre, and not out-of-doors as it would seem. Instead of copying the works of the great masters, Monet preferred looking out the windows of the museum, to study the play of light and colour in the street.*

5. The Garden of l'Infante - 1867. Allen Memorial Art Museum, Oberlin College, Ohio, USA - *This canvas, finished in 1867, was one of several views of Paris that Monet painted during the spring of that year, affirming his preference for working out-of-doors.*

6. Women in the Garden (detail) - 1866-67. Musée d'Orsay, Paris - *Monet first sketched this work in 1866 during his stay in Ville d'Avray and he finished it the following year. The greater part of it was painted out-of-doors, and because the canvas was very large, as he progressively worked up the canvas, he was forced to dig an ever deeper hole to support it. The model for all four women was his mistress Camille.*

7. Jean Monet in his Cradle - 1867. Private collection - *Camille Doncieux and Monet's first child was born on August 8th, 1867. The artist portrayed his son in his cradle, lovingly watched over by Camille, who sat next to him. A bluish light gave the painting the tender intimacy that Monet sought to express.*

8. La Grenouillère - 1869. The Metropolitan Museum of Art, New York. Bequest of Mrs.O. Havemayer, 1929. H.O. Havemayer Collection - *This canvas, painted in 1869, reflects the great friendship that Monet shared with Renoir and the creativity it inspired. With quick brushstrokes, Monet has captured one of the favourite landscapes of the Impressionist painters.*

9. The Jetty at Le Havre - 1868. Private collection - *At the International Maritime Exhibition in Le Havre in 1868, Monet was awarded a medal for the freshness of his canvases representing different views of the region, one of which was this one. The painter was fascinated by the incessant movement of the sea and the boats, as well as the sparkling water reflecting the sky.*

10. The Entrance to the Port at Honfleur - 1867. The Norton Simon Foundation, Los Angeles - *Monet painted this canvas in 1867 during a financially difficult period. Artistically, however, the time was very fertile. The quick rhythm of brushstrokes and the intense vibration of light make it an Impressionist work.*

11. The Voorzaan, near Zaandam - 1871. Private collection - *When the war of 1870 broke out, Monet took his family to London. The following year they moved to Holland. There, on the river Voorzaan, he captured the magic of nature, sparkling with light and infinitely modulated by the delicate tones he brushed onto his canvases.*

12. Windmill near Zaandam - 1871. Private collection - *After leaving Holland, Monet used this motif in many canvases and drawings. This work, finished in 1872, but probably sketched the previous year, perfectly captures the flat Dutch countryside.*

13. The Studio-Boat at Argenteuil - 1874. Kröller-Müller Stichting Museum, Otterlo - *In 1874, Monet painted, like Daubigny before him, the boat where he spent much of his time working, as he floated along the Seine in search of subjects to paint. The reflection on the water and the intense vibration of light made his little studio-boat a perfect observation deck.*

14. Impression, Sunrise - 1873 (dated 1872). Musée de Marmottan, Paris - *After the exhibition of independent artists in Nadar's studio in 1874, this canvas of 1872 became a symbol for that group of painters and gave them their name. It was a synthesis of Monet's style: in it, reality assumes the infinite possibilities that the artist's intuition brings to the image.*

15. The Regatta at Sainte-Adresse - 1867. The Metropolitan Museum of Art, New York. Bequest of William Church, Osborne, 1951 - *Throughout his evolution as an artist, Monet seldom painted human figures. Although there are some included in this work of 1867, the focus is still clearly on nature.*

16. Windmill in Amsterdam - 1874. Private collection - *Monet returned to Holland in 1874 and during his short stay there he painted the streets, canals and windmills of Amsterdam. Using a constantly more refined Impressionist technique, he described his sensations with delicate brushstrokes that were growing ever shorter and more colourful.*

17. Regatta at Argenteuil - 1872. Musée d'Orsay, Paris - *Water was always Monet's favourite subject. He was especially attracted to the Seine and in 1872 he moved to the town of Argenteuil on the river, whose splendid landscape was a powerful source of inspiration for all of the Impressionist painters.*

18. Regatta at Argenteuil, Grey Weather - 1874. Musée du Louvre, Paris - *In this painting done in 1874, one can clearly see how Monet rendered nature the way his sensitive eye saw it, by juxtaposing colours with small fragmented brushstrokes. He coupled complementary colours to reveal perfectly the imperceptible variations of light.*

19. Camille Monet at the Window, Argenteuil - 1873. Private collection - *In this work of 1873, through the arrangement of small coloured brushstrokes that produced almost luminous spots of juxtaposed tonalities, Monet portrayed his wife Camille bathed in an atmosphere of intense light.*

20. Monet's House in Argenteuil - 1876. Private collection - *In his full artistic maturity, Monet succeeded in boldly breaking down pure colour, not only to give importance to it but also to express the vibration of light and to give form to his sensations. In this canvas of 1876 his simple house is transformed by the luminous vibrations.*

21. The Hoschédés' Rose Garden in Mongeron - 1876. Private collection - *The main subject the Impressionists studied was not how to paint objects nor how to use colour. Instead, it was the representation of particular sensations that these colours and objects evoked when they were bathed in the infinite varieties of light.*

22. The Family in the Garden at Argenteuil - 1875. Private collection - *The splendour of Monet's art lies in his intuition that light annulled colour; therefore in his landscapes, the rays of sunlight are dissolved in pure luminosity and objects in shadow come to light, thanks to the intense tonalities of colour.*

23. Gare St.-Lazare - 1877. Musée d'Orsay, Paris - *In this work of 1877, representing a change in Monet's search for subjects, the artist has discovered a new motif. The atmosphere of smoke and steam given off by the train was an inspiration for the painter, who usually perceived the world through the vibrations of the atmosphere.*

24. The Railway Bridge at Argenteuil - 1874. Musée du Louvre, Paris - *For the Impressionists, who loved the countryside around Paris, the many trains passing through the Parisian outskirts were a familiar sight. Monet was particularly struck by the light filtering through the steam and smoke of the locomotive.*

25. Rue St.-Denis, National Holiday - 1878. Musée des Beaux-Arts, Rouen - *The lively character of the happy crowd and the colourful flags fluttering in the streets were caught by Monet in a single moment, marking this canvas as one of the key paintings in Impressionism.*

26. Spring - 1880 (dated 1882). Musée des Arts, Lyon - *Even though this canvas is dated 1882, it was done in 1880 when Monet still lived in Vétheuil, where it seems he found the ideal spot to cultivate the myth of the out-of-doors painter.*

27. Sunset at Lavacourt - 1880. Musée du Petit Palais, Paris - *At the end of the 1880's, when this painting was executed, the Impressionist movement suffered a crisis that split the various painters, sending each one off in his own direction. In spite of this, however, they continued to be linked by a common ideal: freedom of expression.*

28. Etretat, Turbulent Sea - 1883. Musée des Beaux-Arts, Lyon - *The search for new landscapes to inspire him led Monet to move first to Giverny in 1883 and then to the Normandy coast of La Manche where the winter weather caused this dramatic event in nature, captured in this painting.*

29. Under the Lemon Trees in Bordighera - 1884. Ny Carlsberg Glyptotek, Copenhagen - *At the beginning of 1884 Monet visited the Italian Riviera, stopping in Bordighera where he delighted in the colours of the region. His desire to put these colours down on his canvas led him to pursue feverishly the problem of how to do it. By that time, he was making studies that left no room for improvisation.*

30. The Poplars along the Epte - 1891. The Tate Gallery, London - *This was one of the first paintings in his series of poplars painted in 1891 and certainly it was one of the most direct and spontaneous-looking. Successive versions led Monet to an almost obstinate insistence on light over form that took away a certain value from his compositions.*

31. The Poplars - 1891. The Metropolitan Museum of Art, New York - *The serious personal crisis that Monet suffered in 1889, which was not surmounted until 1892 when he married Alice Hoschédé, produced a profound change in him. But it also brought about a certain maturation in his art, for afterwards he abandoned all forms of improvisation.*

32. Morning on the Seine, near Giverny - 1897. Musée du Louvre, Paris - *In this work of 1897 one can already see the precursory signs of a kind of sentimentalism that was pulling Monet, especially towards the end of his life, farther away from the purely visual image of nature.*

33. The Mediterranean near Antibes - 1888. Private collection - *In 1888 the seductive colours of the Mediterranean inspired Monet to paint this work with its sequence of blues and violets, in which the rhythm of the brushstrokes creates a continuity of contrasts between land and sea.*

34. The Cathedral at Rouen, Sunlight - 1894. Musée d'Orsay, Paris - *Monet began a serious study of the effects of light on objects and carried it out through a series of canvases that portrayed the same subject under different effects of light: haystacks, poplars and in this series, the Rouen Cathedral, from 1894.*

35. Parliament, London. Gap of Sunlight in the Fog - 1904. Musée du Louvre, Paris - *At the beginning of the twentieth century Monet returned to places that had inspired him in his youth. In earlier days, he had portrayed everything according to his impression of the moment. Now he painted in a different manner. In this canvas of 1904 the image of London has been completely transformed by his imagination.*

36. Pond of Water Lilies - 1899. Mrs. Albert D. Lasker Collection, New York - *Monet had diverted a tiny river along the edge of his garden to create a small pond that would become, because of its pictorial variety and wealth of details, the dominant theme of his last works.*

37. Water Lilies - 1905. Museum of Fine Arts, Boston. Bequest of Alexander Cochrane - *In his first painting of the pond in 1889, Monet portrayed the trees in the background, the little Japanese bridge and the other aquatic plants. Now, in this painting of 1905 and in the ones that followed, he concentrated on the sparkling surface of the water with its water lilies.*

38. The Church of Santa Maria della Salute, Venice - 1908. Museum of Fine Arts, Boston - *This painting of Venice, plunged in an elusive atmosphere of light and colour, shows how Monet was distancing himself from the reality of his subjects and turning to a more lyrical expression of his emotions.*

39. Water Lilies - 1907. Emil Bürle Collection, Zurich - *In this 1907 version of water lilies even traces of the banks of the pond have disappeared. Only the mirror of water remains, enclosing within its surface the delicate play of light and shadow cast by the surrounding countryside.*

40. Water Lilies - 1910. Kunsthaus, Zurich - *Monet's emotional response to the landscape in his series of water lilies, which led him to depict them in soft tones or, as in this canvas of 1910, in a riot of colour, reflect the changes in his spirit.*

41. Water Lilies - 1907. Private collection - *The unbelievable exultation of Monet's imagination created a mixture, in a single image, of sky and water, giving the surface of the pond in this version from 1907, a light worthy of the most daring romantic visions.*

42. Reflections in the Water (center section) - c. 1917. Musée Léon Alègre, Bagnols-sur-Cèze - *The astonishing technique and the complete mastery of his means may have stood in the way of Monet's search for subjects, for they were often approached with a certain preciousness. This canvas, with its unreal transparency, dates from 1917.*

43. Willows, Giverny - 1918. Private collection - *When Monet painted this willow in his garden, in 1918, he went beyond the limits of reality, giving nature all the unbelievable colours of his passion and his imagination.*

44. Garden at Giverny - Musée de peinture et de sculpture, Grenoble - *In the forms of his compositions, in the creative invention of colour and in the image embraced by an imaginary nature, Monet seems in his last works to be almost a precursor of modern painting.*

1. *Shipyard near Honfleur* - 1864. Private collection

3. *Camille or The Green Dress* - 1866. Kunsthalle, Bremen

2. *Luncheon on the Grass* (detail from the left half) - 1866, Musée d'Orsay, Paris

4. *The Church of Saint-Germain-l'Auxerrois, Paris* - 1867 (dated 1866).
   Nationalgalerie, Charlottenburg, West Berlin

5. *The Garden of l'Infante* - 1867. Allen Memorial Art Museum, Oberlin College, Ohio, USA

6. *Women in the Garden* (detail) - 1866-67. Musée d'Orsay, Paris

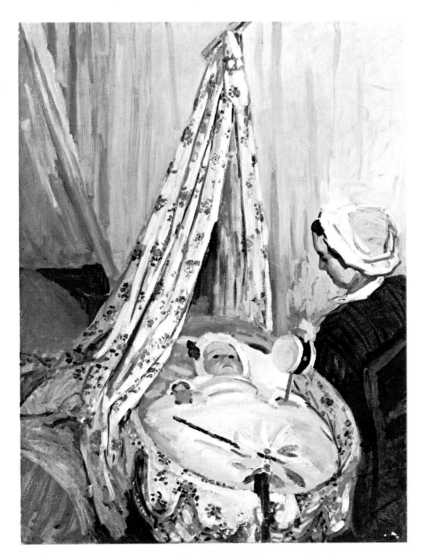

7. *Jean Monet in his Cradle* - 1867. Private collection

8. *La Grenouillère* - 1869. The Metropolitan Museum of Art,
New York. Bequest of Mrs. O. Havemayer, 1929.
H.O. Havemayer Collection

9. *The Jetty at Le Havre* - 1868. Private collection

10. *The Entrance to the Port at Honfleur* - 1867. The Norton Simon Foundation, Los Angeles

11. *The Voorzaan, near Zaandam* - 1871. Private collection

12. *Windmill near Zaandam* - 1871. Private collection

13. *The Studio-Boat at Argenteuil* - 1874. Kröller-Müller Stichting, Otterlo

14. *Impression, Sunrise* - 1873 (dated 1872). Musée de Marmottan, Paris

15. *The Regatta at Sainte-Adresse* - 1867. The Metropolitan Museum of Art, New York. Bequest of William Church, Osborne, 1951

16. *Windmill in Amsterdam* - 1874. Private collection

17. *Regatta at Argenteuil* - 1872. Musée d'Orsay, Paris

18. *Regatta at Argenteuil, Grey Weather* - 1874. Musée du Louvre, Paris

19. *Camille Monet at the Window, Argenteuil* - 1873. Private collection

20. *Monet's House in Argenteuil* - 1876. Private collection

21. *The Hoschédés' Rose Garden in Mongeron* - 1876. Private collection

23. *Gare St.-Lazare* - 1877. Musée d'Orsay, Paris

26. *Spring* - 1880 (dated 1882). Musée des Arts, Lyon

27. *Sunset at Lavacourt* - 1880. Musée du Petit Palais, Paris

28. *Etretat, Turbulent Sea* - 1883. Musée des Beaux-Arts, Lyon

29. *Under the Lemon Trees in Bordighera* - 1884. Ny Carlsberg Glyptotek, Copenhagen

30. *The Poplars along the Epte* - 1891. The Tate Gallery, London

31. *The Poplars* - 1891. The Metropolitan Museum of Art, New York

32. *Morning on the Seine, near Giverny* - 1897. Musée du Louvre, Paris

33. *The Mediterranean near Antibes* - 1888. Private collection

34. *The Cathedral at Rouen, Sunlight* - 1894. Musée d'Orsay, Paris

35. *Parliament, London. Gap of Sunlight in the Fog* - 1904. Musée du Louvre, Paris

36. *Pond of Water Lilies* - 1899. Mrs Albert D. Lasker Collection, New York

37. *Water Lilies* - 1905. Museum of Fine Arts, Boston. Bequest of Alexander Cochrane

38. *The Church of Santa Maria della Salute, Venice* - 1908.
    Museum of Fine Arts, Boston

39. *Water Lilies* - 1907. Emil Bürle Collection, Zurich

40. *Water Lilies* - 1910. Kunsthaus, Zurich

41. *Water Lilies* - 1907. Private collection

42. *Reflections in the Water* (center section) - c. 1917. Musée Léon Alègre, Bagnols-sur-Cèze

43. *Willows, Giverny* - 1918. Private collection

44. *Garden at Giverny* - Musée de peinture et de sculpture, Grenoble

Editor in chief Anna Maria Mascheroni

Art director Luciano Raimondi

Text Alberta Melanotte

Translation Kerry Milis

Production Art, Bologna

Photos Credits Gruppo Editoriale Fabbri S.p.A., Milan

Published by Park Lane
An Imprint of Grange Books
The Grange
Grange Yard
LONDON
SE1 3AG

ISBN 1-85627-195-1

This edition reprinted 1993

Printed in Italy by Gruppo Editoriale Fabbri S.p.A., Milan